NEWPORT

1. Hanging Rock
2. St. Georges School
3. Narragansett Bay
4. Newport Bridge
5. Cliff Walk
6. Rough Point
7. Castle Hill
8. Castle Hill Lighthouse
9. Goat Island
10. Bowen's Wharf
11. Trinity Church
12. Touro Synagogue
13. Colony House
14. Miramar
15. The Breakers
16. International Tennis Hall of Fame
17. Astor's Beechwood
18. New York Yacht Club
19. Common Burial Ground
20. International Yacht Restoration School
21. Goat Island Lighthouse (Green Light)
22. Newport naval base
23. Brenton Cove
24. Bannister's Wharf
25. Sachuest Beach
26. Newport Harbor
27. Fort Adams State Park
28. Rose Island

ISBN-13: 978-1-889833-63-7

Library of Congress Cataloging-in-Publication Data
Nesbitt, Alexander.
  Newport / photographs by Alexander Nesbitt ; text by Molly Sexton.
     p. cm. — (New England landmarks)
  ISBN 1-889833-63-0
  1. Newport (R.I.)—Pictorial works. 2. Newport (R.I.)—Description and travel. I. Sexton, Molly. II. Title. III. Series.
  F89.N5N38 2005
  917.45'70444—dc22   2005012286

Cover and interior design by Peter Blaiwas, Vern Associates, Inc.
Layout by Benjamin Jenness, Vern Associates, Inc.
Map on endpapers by Jeffery M. Walsh
Printed in South Korea.

Commonwealth Editions
266 Cabot Street, Beverly, Massachusetts 01915
www.commonwealtheditions.com

Front cover: Schooner *America* (replica of the original America's Cup winner) sailing out of
            Newport Harbor
Back cover: Gaslights, Queen Anne's Square and Trinity Church

The New England Landmarks Series
Cape Cod National Seashore, photographs by Andrew Borsari
Walden Pond, photographs by Bonnie McGrath
Revolutionary Sites of Greater Boston, photographs by Ulrike Welsch
Boston Harbor Islands, photographs by Sherman Morss Jr.
Providence, photographs by Richard Benjamin

Newport

PHOTOGRAPHS BY ALEXANDER NESBITT

Text by Molly Sexton

NEW ENGLAND LANDMARKS

COMMONWEALTH EDITIONS
Beverly, Massachusetts

*I*slands foster fierce independence on one hand and demand generous cooperation on the other. On an island, we are both alone and together. We are separated from other places and other people, from everything that is not here. Even the sun's light seems to have to cross the water to reach us each morning and each evening.

On islands large and small, with bridges or without, things often feel manageably small, intimate. One knows, "We are all that is here, and the sea might wash us away one day." Without judgment or care, the tides wear inexorably at our coast, altering the topography, shaving the edges ever fractionally closer to us. We stand closer together. We need each other on an island. Perhaps that is why people have always found them romantic.

"Aquidneck," the name of this island when it was purchased in 1637 from the Native Americans who lived here, simply means "island" in Algonquit. For over five thousand years before the colonists came, people summered here—fishing the waters, clearing the land, and nourishing the soil with seaweed gathered from the shore. It was then and remains today a place with a beautiful, safe, natural harbor, good fertile earth, and a refreshing summer breeze.

Guarded by a rocky coast that rears 188 feet out of the seabed and embraced by rhythmic waves forever kissing the shore, Aquidneck's 39 square miles of ground reveal themselves to be what many islands are: a staunch and pleasant land, both outpost and harbor.

(*overleaf*) Looking west from Hanging Rock with St. George's School on the horizon

Jumping from the Dumplings in the east passage of Narragansett Bay,
with Clingstone House and Newport Bridge beyond

I LIKE TO WALK HOME BY THE CLIFF WALK,
and as I never can break off when once
I've begun it, I generally end up by doing
all four miles. I bring a book along and
read a hundred pages in every one of my
favorite retreats, while the sun goes
down and the almost-Italian sea goes
through a series of enchanting metamor-
phoses between its headlands and rocks.

—Thornton Wilder, Newport, 1922

Cliff Walk from the lawn of Rough Point

Looking north up the east passage from Castle Hill Lighthouse

FROM THAT MAGICAL ROOM I could see at night the beacons of six lighthouses and hear the booming and chiming of as many sea buoys.

—Thornton Wilder, *Theophilus North*

IF IT IS TRUE THAT ENVIRONMENT shapes and molds the human character, then Narragansett Bay has provided an environment through the years which has exerted a powerful force on the lives of generations of Rhode Islanders. Present inhabitants of the nation's smallest state, while no longer as dependent on the Bay for the necessities and luxuries of life as were their predecessors, retain deep, often subconscious, attachment to their link with the open sea.

—Stuart O. Hale,
Narragansett Bay: A Friend's Perspective

Lagoon on Ocean Drive, with Seafair in the distance

Newport was settled by revolutionary spiritual thinkers who followed a remarkable woman named Anne Hutchinson out of Puritan Boston. As a matter of both survival and idealism, Newport's founders brought a tolerant and independent spirit that is well suited to both outcasts and islands. The values embedded in Newport's first documents—"liberty of conscience and religion"—drew diverse yet like-minded settlers. Together they built one of the world's first democracies with separated church and state and an explicit policy of religious tolerance. Jews, Quakers, Seventh Day Baptists, and Anglicans built some of their first North American churches here; they came from the Caribbean, South America, Africa, and England and as exiles from colonies where they were in danger of being whipped or even hanged for dissension.

Today regarded as a small city by most standards, Newport was once one of the five leading ports in the New World, competing with Boston, Charleston, Philadelphia, and New York for international trade. Newport resisted outside pressures in setting up its social and commercial covenants. Newporters flaunted British oversight. Tax agents of the Crown were hanged in effigy or driven out by rioters who tore apart and burned their vessels.

The name "Rhode Island" was punned into "Rogue's Island." It was a radical place. The Declaration of Independence, just days off the hand presses in Philadelphia, was read aloud from the balcony of Newport's Colony House on the Parade.

Tolerance had its limits, however. Jews were denied the vote until the late eighteenth century. Although slave importation stopped around the same time and children of slave women were declared free born, Newport merchants persisted in the trade in other American ports. Some Newport slaves bought their freedom and fared relatively well as independent tradespeople. They began a free, if small, African American culture here long before it was possible to do so in most other American places.

Newport was most often progressive. It was the first American city to establish a land grant endowment for the education of the poor. During the brutal King Philip's War (1675–1676) that erupted between Native Americans and colonists, Newport was the only warfare-free zone for refugees. The charter granted by the crown in the 1660s was perhaps the most lenient ever issued. Until the 1840s that document served not just the City of Newport but eventually the state of Rhode Island as its Constitution.

Newport skyline from Goat Island

THE MOST SERIOUS CHARGE

which can be brought

against New England is not

Puritanism but February.

—Joseph Wood Krutch

Trinity Church through cherry blossoms

Touro Synagogue

THE CITIZENS OF THE UNITED STATES OF AMERICA
have a right to applaud themselves for having
given to mankind examples of an enlarged and
liberal policy: a policy worthy of imitation. All
possess alike liberty of conscience and immunities
of citizenship. . . . For happily the Government of
the United States, which gives to bigotry no sanc-
tion, to persecution no assistance, requires only
that they who live under its protection should
demean themselves as good citizens. . . . May the
children of the Stock of Abraham, who dwell in
this land, continue to merit and enjoy the good
will of the other inhabitants, while every one
shall sit in safety under his own vine and fig-tree,
and there shall be none to make him afraid.

—George Washington, letter to the Hebrew
    congregation of Newport, 1790

LAST NIGHT A PARTY OF REBELS LANDED BEHIND GENERAL SMITH'S LATE QUARTERS at Redwood, from whence they advanced to General Prescott's quarters . . . They laid hold of Genl. Prescott and carried him off, also Lieut. Barrington, his aide . . . The Rebels certainly ran a great risk in making this attempt. They, however, executed it in a masterly manner. It is certainly a most extraordinary circumstance that a General commanding a body of 4,000 men, encamped on an Island surrounded by a squadron of Ships of War should be carried from his quarters at night by a small party of the enemy, and without a shot being fired.

—From the diary of Frederick MacKenzie, a British soldier
    stationed in Newport at the time of the Revolution

Balcony of the Colony House, from which the Declaration
of Independence was first read to Rhode Islanders

Newport's early houses of worship represent significant diversity and religious tolerance. They also testify to the exemplary skill of the well-known master builders who created them. The Friends Meeting House (1699), Trinity Church (built in 1725 for a congregation begun in 1698), Seventh Day Baptist Church (1730), and Touro Synagogue (1763) are internationally-recognized examples of the period when master builders reigned supreme, and Architecture with a capital A was yet unknown in the colonies.

By the mid-1800s Newport had firmly established itself as a fashionable resort town, and by the 1870s there was no place like it in the world for a summer vacation. The Gilded Age mansions of Bellevue Avenue, built as retreats from the summer heat of big cities, are unequaled for their grandeur or their number. For a few short decades around the turn of the twentieth century the world's most illustrious architects, designers, artisans, and hosts strove to outdo one another in marble, gilt, and luxury. Now nearly a million people each year come to Newport to spend a few hours inside these showplaces.

But the truly remarkable thing about Newport is that both the opulent and the ordinary have been lovingly preserved here. The Point District's baseball park, Cardine's Field, is not a spectacular structure like Bellevue Avenue's International Tennis Hall of Fame, but it is one of the oldest urban ballparks in America. Through the foresight of non-profit organizations and dedicated citizens—and through being overlooked by developers who did so much architectural damage to New England towns after World War II—Newport today has more vernacular colonial homes than any other town in America.

We are at home in yesterday here. We live not just in the shadow of great marble houses, but within the lath and plaster walls of America's original middle class. We worship in the same churches and cook in the same kitchens and grow herbs in the same dooryards; we walk the same streets in the winter wind, and duck into the same taverns for a drink. It happens often in Newport—turn a cobbled corner on a snowy evening, pass through the umbra of a gas streetlight, catch sight of the masts of old ships still afloat in the harbor, and one's sureness of the date falters.

Fountain at Miramar,
from Bellevue Avenue

Marble House, from Bellevue Avenue

NEWPORT IS THE MOST BEAUTIFUL OF PLACES.
I find here a splendor of houses, a refine-
ment of life that I have scarcely seen else-
where. . . . There are few centres of
civilization that I do not know, but here in
Newport, I find everything combined—the
luxury of Paris, the art of Italy, the hospi-
tality of the East, and the natural beauty
of the Riviera.

—Paul Charles Joseph Bourget, 1893

FOR FORTY YEARS OR SO this was the world headquarters of conspicuous consumption.

—Bill Bryson,
The Lost Continent, 1999

Tour guide at The Breakers

ONE HUNDRED YEARS AFTER THE DECLARATION that all men are created equal, there began to gather in Newport a colony of the rich, determined to show that some Americans were conspicuously more equal than others.

—Alistair Cooke, *America*

(overleaf) Grass court at the International Tennis Hall of Fame

An exhibition in period tennis garb at the International Tennis Hall of Fame

Veranda of the Astors' Beechwood, from Cliff Walk

WE ALL OF US KNOW TOWNS LIKE THESE.
I personally know four. One is in Belgium, one in Switzerland, one in the Far West of the United States. The fourth is here, where I live. None of these communities have today anything in common except that intangible quality called character. They are eternally themselves, and therefore indestructible.

—Arthur Tuckerman,
  When Rochambeau Stepped Ashore

THE INHABITANT OF AN ISLAND CAN TELL
what currents formed the land which he
cultivates; and his earth is still being
created or destroyed. There before his
door, perchance, still empties the stream
which brought down the material of his
farm ages before, and is still bringing it
down or washing it away,—the graceful,
gentle robber!

—Henry David Thoreau, 1849

(*overleaf*) Newport home of the New York Yacht Club

Colonial doorway, Spring Street

IT HAPPENS TO BE ONE OF THOSE STRANGE, ODD LITTLE CORNERS of the earth which defy time because they are somehow greater than the successive human generations which inhabit them.

—Arthur Tuckerman, *When Rochambeau Stepped Ashore*

Thames Street

FOR A WHILE I THOUGHT NEWPORT WAS THE ONLY PLACE there could be a jazz festival, like the Indianapolis 500 can only happen in Indianapolis. But just like there are NASCAR races all over now, jazz festivals have proliferated. Today there are more than 1,000 jazz festivals worldwide.

—George Wein, founder and producer,
    Newport Jazz Festival

Herbie Hancock, Newport Jazz Festival fiftieth anniversary, 2004

The New England seashore has such a hold on the American imagination that Disney World has dedicated an entire themed resort to it. Heritage sites and cultural tourism are multi-billion dollar industries, as is recreation. What does work mean in a place where so many come to play?

Entire professions have been kept alive by the constant task of honoring Newport's particular character. In 1675, in the fading afternoon light, someone went to work, probably on foot, to tend bar at the White Horse Tavern. And someone is likely doing the very same today. At the John Stevens Shop, stone carvers have chipped away at headstones since 1705. Along the wharves of Lower Thames Street, dozens of student apprentices still learn the traditional techniques of wooden boat building. There have been carpenters, merchants, doctors, and dentists, undertakers, innkeepers, immigrants, pharmacists, and fishermen at work on these cobbled streets and pebbled beaches for over 350 years, passing along their trades and secrets, and adapting to new economies.

For a time the U.S. Navy kept Newport afloat. During World War II, about fourteen thousand workers per day traveled by boat to the torpedo station on Goat Island. Today that munitions plant is closed and Goat Island has a causeway, a marina, a hotel, and spectacular views of the harbor and city. Rose Island, a fort in the eighteenth century and a tended lighthouse and munitions storage site until the mid-twentieth, is now a non-profit working lighthouse and guesthouse. Staying relevant in changing circumstances means always entertaining fresh possibilities.

For this reason, resort towns have secret places, routes, and lexicons about which visitors are not told: it is a way to keep things fresh. That need for freshness, for revising perspective and examining different possibilities, may be why so many artists live and work here. Newport offers a legacy of things made over time and with care, an inspirational land and seascape, and an active nexus of creativity. It is a place where work and play fit together.

AT HIS SHOP on the north end of Thames Street any persons may be supplied with tomb-stones, grave-stones, hearth and printers press-stones, and . . . every kind of work in stone is performed in the neatest and most elegant manner. . . . All sorts of country produce, or West-India and dry goods, will be taken pay for said work.

—Advertisement for the
John Stevens Shop, 1781

Interior, John Stevens Shop, Thames Street

THE VERY NAMES RECORDED HERE ARE STRANGE,

Of foreign accent, and of different climes;

Alvares and Rivera interchange

With Abraham and Jacob of old times.

—Henry Wadsworth Longellow,

"The Jewish Cemetery at Newport"

Headstone, Colonial Burying Ground

COMBINE! YE SONS OF FREEDOM, AH, COMBINE!

The people are invincible, who join:

Factions and feuds will overturn the state,

Which union renders flourishing and great.

—John Stevens III, 1770

(overleaf) Beetle Cat hulls being rebuilt at International Yacht Restoration School (IYRS)

Crew from Aquidneck Lobster Company hauling a trap fishing net

(*overleaf*) Newfoundland fishing dory *Savage* passing
Goat Island Lighthouse ("The Green Light")

The 12-meter yacht *Intrepid* passing the aircraft
carrier *Saratoga* at Newport naval base

Every sort of vessel passes through this harbor. There are tall ships and schooners, pea pods and beetle cats, sloops, yawls, ketches, and smacks. There are draggers and dories, picnic boats, ferries and tugboats, with barges pushing up the bay amidst cruise ships and kayaks. There are wooden masts and carbon-fiber hulls moored side by side with steel research vessels. The longest winning streak in the history of sports is America's defense of the America's Cup, the oldest trophy in sport. For over fifty years that drama played itself out here. To this day, over twenty years after the Cup was lost, Newport Harbor is home to the largest fleet of 12-meter racing yachts in the world.

And there is every sort of mariner here as well. There are motor boaters and oarsmen, those who sail for a living, those who live for sailing, and those whose only concern is fish. There are professionals and weekenders.

There are sailors without land legs and some without legs at all. In the shadow of the racing 12-meters on a summer afternoon, one can often see the Optis—tiny little boats sailed by kids as young as six—rounding their own small bright marks in fluttering clusters, tiny sea-borne butterflies.

Whether or not our livelihoods are linked to the sea, in living here we learn from those who do depend upon it. We know the ways of surfers and fishermen and sailors and ocean scientists; we are familiar with their passions and concerns. Even those who never learn to swim know how our buoyant bodies feel in the salty sea and the way sand works its way to the roots of your hair in the wind. We all know the strength of hurricanes and the frailty of warm days in the early spring. We know lobster and little-necks and butter and fog, and we know that a walk on the beach can turn a bad day around, like a shift in the wind.

ALL OF US HAVE IN OUR VEINS THE EXACT SAME PERCENTAGE OF SALT in our blood that exists in the ocean, and therefore we have salt in our blood, in our sweat, in our tears. We are tied to the ocean. And when we go back to the sea—whether it is to sail or to watch it—we are going back from whence we came.

—John Fitzgerald Kennedy, 1962

From the masthead of the 12-meter yacht *Nefertiti*

BELIEVE ME, MY YOUNG FRIEND, THERE IS NOTHING—
absolutely nothing—half so much worth doing as
simply messing about in boats.

—Kenneth Grahame, *The Wind in the Willows,* 1908

Skipper of the schooner *Adirondack*

Match race between 2003 America's Cup winner *Alinghi* (right) and U.S. challenger *Oracle*

YOU ARE ON THE WATERS OF THE FINEST BAY IN THE WORLD.

World travelers say so. I say so. Do not argue about facts.

—George C. Hull, *Providence Journal-Bulletin*

A TOURIST REMAINS AN OUTSIDER THROUGHOUT HIS VISIT, but a sailor is part of the local scene from the moment he arrives.

—Ann Davison, first woman to cross
the Atlantic single-handed

Crew members on the boom of a 12-meter yacht, enjoying a fun sail

Fleet of Optimus class dinghies ("Optis") from Sail Newport Sailing School, in Brenton Cove

Lobster boats tied up at the pier

[THE SOUTHWEST WIND] IS THE PLEASINGEST, warmest wind in the Climate, most desired of the Indians, making faire weather ordinarily; and therefore they have a Tradition, that to the Southwest, which they call Sowwaniu, the gods chiefly dwell; and hither the soules of all their Great and Good men and women goe.

—Roger Williams, 1643

AT ANY TIME THE DISPLAY OF LIGHTS THAT AT NIGHT ARE STATIONARY along the wharves or upon the vessel at anchor or dart to and fro, Meteor–like, amid more stable constellations, affords a spectacle of unusual attractiveness; but when the vessels are multiplied and the lights increased a thousand fold; when, instead of hulls that adorn the bosom of the harbor, there is a continuous blaze of kaleidoscopic radiance from a countless multitude of craft, that lie so close that it seems as through the harbor had disappeared, then one sees the water side of Newport in its supreme glory.

—Edgar Mayhew Bacon, 1904

Bannister's and Bowen's wharves during Tall Ships 2000

Sunset walk at Sachuest Beach, with St. George's School beyond

WHEN I WAS A BOY GROWING UP, MY GREATEST ASPIRATION was to come to Rhode Island to play in the Newport Jazz Festival. . . . When I was sixteen, I thought that would be the measure of my success. I couldn't have dreamed I'd become President. I thought, if I could just play one time in the Newport Jazz Festival, I would know I had arrived.

—President William Jefferson Clinton, 1998

ACKNOWLEDGMENTS

These photographs were years in the making. I could never have steered that course alone, and as a result there are many, many people to thank. I have to start with thanking my father, Alexander Nesbitt, for imparting his drive and love of books; my mother, Ilse, for her great depth of love, support, and wisdom; and my brother, Rupert, for his endless brilliant counsel—no brother has a better sounding board. There are so many friends to thank for years of unwavering faith and support: I hope you all know to include yourselves. Molly Sexton has been a joy to work with over the years both in my own business and on numerous other efforts. I have always been charmed by her writing, so she was an instant first choice for this project. My photographer friends also deserve a special thanks, particularly Richard Benjamin, Onne van der Wal, Rob van Petten, Clint Clemens, and Mike Eudenbach.

ALEXANDER "SANDY" NESBITT is a native of Newport and a 1990 graduate of Pratt Institute in Brooklyn, New York. As a freelance photographer, he has traveled and worked widely, from the Middle East and southern Africa to the Caribbean and Mexico. He regularly returns to shoot everything around his home in Newport, where he maintains his studio and storefront, Blink Gallery.

Photo by Maaike Bernström

MOLLY SEXTON is a native of Saunderstown, Rhode Island. A freelance writer, she has been named one of Rhode Island's most influential people in the arts by the *Providence Phoenix*. She lives in Newport.

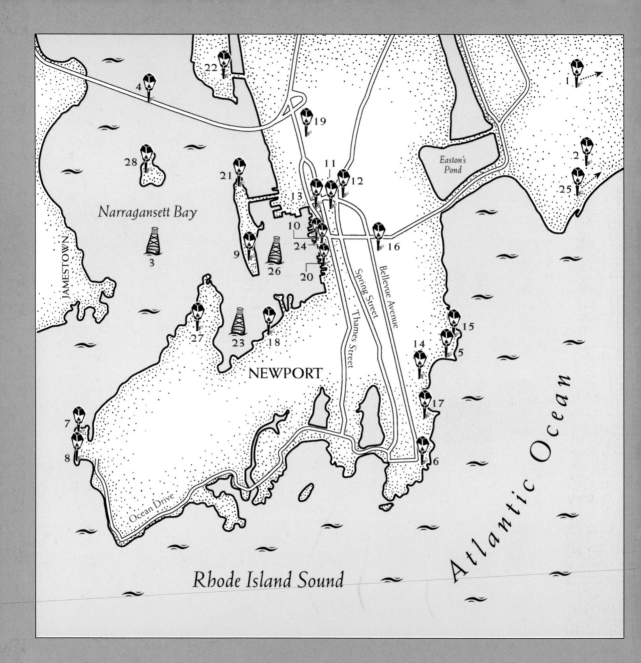

Contents

Words printed in **bold letters like these**
are explained in the Glossary.

What is a temple?

A temple is a building where **Hindus** come to worship. Hindus follow the religion called **Hinduism**, which comes from India. Hinduism is the oldest religion in the world. It goes back more than 5000 years.

An Indian word for temple is **mandir**. A mandir is a special place where Hindus can feel close to **God**.

Some Hindu temples are small and simple. Others, like this one, are large and often covered with beautiful carvings. Large, old temples, like this one, are usually found in India.

Hindu people in Britain

Many Hindus have come to Britain over the last 50 years. Some came from India. Others moved to Britain from East Africa.

When Hindu people first came to Britain most of them were not very rich. They could not afford to build their own temples. They bought old buildings and turned them into temples.

Many Hindus moved from India and East Africa to Britain.

This temple is in South London. It was one of the first to be opened in Britain. The building used to be a church.

Temples in Britain

There are many different types of **mandir**. Some are in the town and some in the countryside. Some are old buildings, some are new ones.

This temple has a small farm with bulls and cows. The farm provides food and milk for the temple.

Orange flags

In Britain, many **Hindu** temples look just like other buildings. You can tell what they are by the orange flag that often flies from the roof.

New temples

Hindu people in Britain have begun to build their own mandirs. Some new temples are built to look like old Hindu temples in India. Others are built in a modern style.

This modern temple is in Leicester.

Where to find Hindu temples

There are over 150 temples in Britain. Most Hindu people live around London or Leicester. Others live around Birmingham, Manchester and other large cities and towns.

This mandir is in North London. It looks like some of the temples in India and is made from marble.

What's inside?

Visitors to the temple take off their shoes before going in. This is to show respect and to keep the temple clean. There are special racks to put your shoes on.

When you enter the temple you may notice the smell of **incense**. Incense is a perfume which is burned to make a pleasant scent.

There are often many rooms in a **mandir**. There are usually offices, a kitchen and a dining area, as well as a room for **worship**.

Worshippers remove their shoes before going into a temple.

The temple room

When Hindus enter the main temple room they ring a bell hanging from the ceiling. Then they stand in front of a **shrine** and offer prayers to the **murtis**. The murtis are sacred **images** of the Hindu **gods** and **goddesses** inside the shrine.

After praying, worshippers leave gifts of money, rice, fruit or flowers for the gods and goddesses in the shrine. Then they may sip a few drops of **holy water**.

A Hindu woman offers prayers to a shrine. You can see the gifts of flowers in front of the murtis.

The shrine

Only **priests** are allowed into the **shrine** itself.
The priests look after the **murtis** with love and
devotion. They clean and dress them each morning.
You cannot usually see this because the curtains in
front of the shrine are closed at such times.

Priests also offer the murtis **vegetarian** food.
After it has been offered to the murtis, it is
called **prashad**. This **holy** food is given to visitors.

This priest is **worshipping** murtis in the temple shrine.

God, gods and goddesses

Hindus worship many different murtis. Some are thought to be **God**. Others are lesser **gods** and **goddesses**. Hindus believe they have great power over the universe.

There are three main gods and goddesses: **Vishnu**, **Shiva** and **Durga**. **Krishna** is another name for Vishnu. You can see him on page 10. He is often shown playing a flute.

A painting of Shiva carrying a trident, drum and water pot.

Shiva's wife is called Durga. In this murti she is shown riding a lion.

Worship in the temple

In the temple, some people **worship** alone. Most take **darshan**, which is when they stand before the **murtis** and offer prayers. They may also chant **mantras**, counting them on a string of beads. A mantra is a short prayer which is said again and again.

The arti ceremony

Some worship is performed in groups. The most important ceremony is called **arti**. A lamp, a flower, **incense** and water are offered to the murti. The lamp and the flower are then passed around the **congregation**.

The arti lamp is passed around worshippers, who either stand or sit cross-legged on the floor.

Other types of worship

There are other ways **Hindus** worship together.
One is the **sacred-fire ceremony**. It is often
performed at special events, such as weddings.
(You can see a picture of this ceremony on page 18.)

Listening to readings from the **holy** books is another
form of worship. Hindus have many different holy
books. The oldest are called the **Vedas**. For many
Hindus the **Bhagavad Gita** (The Song of **God**) is the
most important.

Holy books

Some Hindu holy books
praise God, some tell
people how to worship,
and others are about
Hindu beliefs. Many
of them are written
in **Sanskrit**.

A **priest** talking to
people in a temple
in Southall, London.

Festivals

The temple is very busy on festival days. There are many festivals during the year. For most **Hindus**, the main one is **Divali**, the Hindu New Year. At Divali the temple is decorated with rows of candles or lights.

At most festivals special stories are told. There is music, singing and dancing. It is a time for fun and celebration.

Girls and women perform a stick-dance during the **Navaratri** festival.

Festival food

On many festivals Hindus **fast**. This means that they go without food for some time. This is followed by feasting. Most food eaten at festivals is **vegetarian**.

Janmashtami is a festival that celebrates **Krishna's** birthday. On this day some Hindus fast until midnight, when Krishna was born. Then there is a beautiful **arti** ceremony followed by a feast.

Festival food

Here are just a few of the special foods eaten at Hindu festivals: puris are flat round breads fried in ghee (oil made from butter); samosas are pastries stuffed with vegetables; burfi is a kind of fudge made from sugar and milk.

These Hindu women are preparing festival food in a temple kitchen.

Music and art

Music is very important to **Hindus**. Hindu songs of **worship** are called **bhajans**. They are sung during the **arti** ceremony and at festivals. They are often sung in **Hindi** or another Indian language.

These are the main instruments played during festivals or worship. Tablas are drums you play with the hands. Hand cymbals are used to keep the rhythm (beat). The harmonium is a small organ pumped by hand.

Hindu musicians playing during a wedding celebration. You can see the tablas (drums) in the left of the picture.

16

Temple pictures

In a Hindu temple you can see paintings or pictures of the different **gods** and **saints**. They are very brightly coloured. You will also see different **symbols** connected with **Hinduism**.

Hindu symbols

This symbol is called **Aum**. It represents Hinduism. You say the word as if it were written 'Ah-oo-m'.

This is a swastika. It is a sign of good luck.

This is a picture of the god **Ganesha**. He has an elephant's head. He is the son of **Shiva**.

We listen to music with our ears. We see pictures with our eyes. Can you find out how Hindus use their nose, tongue and sense of touch in worship?
You can find the answers on page 23.

The temple and the people

The temple is not just for **worship**. It is also a place where **Hindus** meet together for fun, celebrations and to help others.

Many Hindu families use the temple for special events. These include weddings and the name-giving ceremony for babies.

Some events are performed outside the temple, often at home. For these ceremonies, such as funerals, the **priest** comes from the **mandir**.

The **sacred-fire ceremony** performed during a wedding at a mandir.

Helping others

In Britain, the temple is also a **community** centre.
Rooms are used for meetings and for teaching.
There may be a large hall for putting on Indian
music, dance and theatre. The building is used as a
base to assist the poor, old people and others who
need help. Some temples help feed the homeless.

Hindus believe that special
care should be given to
children, women, animals
(especially cows), **holy**
people and old people.
Hindus believe that if these
five groups are cared for
God will be pleased and
everyone will be happy.

This dance in Leicester is
part of a charity event.

The home as a temple

Hindus believe that the home should also be a temple. Every Hindu house has its own **shrine**. This may simply be a few pictures on a shelf. Sometimes it may take up a whole room. The shrine usually has **images** or pictures of one or more of the **gods** and **goddesses**.

In **Hinduism** there is no special day of the week for **worship**. Hindus usually worship at least once a day. Early morning before dawn is thought to be the best time. It is very calm and peaceful then.

A Hindu family worshipping at a shrine in their home.

Learning about Hinduism

Hindu children learn by taking part in worship at home. They may help their parents during the **arti** ceremony.

Children also learn by hearing stories from their parents or grandparents. Sometimes when they are playing they may even pretend to be **Krishna**, **Shiva** or **Durga**. By remembering **God**, the home also becomes a temple. It is a very special place.

Sometimes Hindu children have their own small shrines. Here a Hindu girl is praying to Krishna.

Glossary

The letters in brackets help you to say each word.

arti (ar-tee) main ceremony in Hindu temples

Aum (om) symbol which is often used to represent Hinduism

Bhagavad Gita (buh-guh-vud gee-tuh) one of the most important and popular Hindu holy books

bhajan (buh-juhn) Hindu song of worship; a song in praise of God

community a group of people; the people who live in the neighbourhood

congregation the group of people who come to the church, mosque or temple

darshan (dar-shun) coming before the murti; seeing the murti

Divali (dee-var-lee) one of the main Hindu festivals. For most Hindus it is the New Year celebration.

Durga (doo-r-guh) the main Hindu goddess; the wife of Shiva

fast to go without food for some time for religious reasons

Ganesha (gun-esh) a Hindu god. One of the sons of Shiva and Durga.

God the Greatest person; the highest of the gods. Krishna (or Vishnu) is often thought to be God, and sometimes Shiva.

god a male being believed to have great power over human lives

goddess a female being believed to have great power over human lives

Hindi the main official language of India

Hinduism the main religion of India

Hindus followers of the religion of Hinduism

holy means respected because it is to do with God

holy water water which has been specially blessed

image picture or holy statue of a god or goddess

incense perfume which is burned to make a pleasant smell

Janmashtami (juhn-mush-tuh-mee) Hindu festival held on Krishna's birthday

Krishna (krish-nuh) one of the main Hindu gods

mandir (mun-deer) Indian word for temple

mantra (mun-truh) prayer; a string of holy words

murti (moo-r-tee) a form or image of a god or goddess usually made of wood, metal or marble

Navaratri (nuh-vuh-ruh-tree) festival held in honour of Durga. It lasts for nine days.

prashad (pruh-shard) sacred food; food offered to God

priests people who lead worship

sacred-fire ceremony Hindu ceremony where grains are thrown into a fire

Sanskrit (sann-skrit) very old language once spoken in India

saint someone who lives an especially good religious life

Shiva (shiver) one of the main Hindu gods

shrine holy place where people worship

symbol sign with a special meaning

Vedas (vay-duhs) the oldest Hindu holy books. They contain the basic truths which Hindus believe never change.

vegetarian food which does not have meat in it

Vishnu (vish-noo) one of the main Hindu gods

worship show respect and love for God, saints or anything which is holy

Answers to questions on page 17:
Hindus use the nose to smell the **incense** and flowers offered to God. The tongue is used to taste **prashad**. The sense of touch is used when chanting on meditation beads.

Index